Made in United States
North Haven, CT
04 August 2022

22231166R00074